FAIRACRES PUBL

THE MONASTIC HOURS OF PRAYER

BENEDICTA WARD SLG

SLG Press
Convent of the Incarnation
Fairacres Parker Street
Oxford OX4 1TB
www.slgpress.co.uk

ISBN: 978-0-7283-0283-9 (Print)
ISBN: 978-0-7283-0284-6 (ePub)
ISBN: 978-0-7283-0285-3 (MOBI)

Cover Image: Illuminated letter B from the first word of Psalm 1, The Luttrell Psalter, Add. 42130, f.13. © The British Library Board, used with permission.

Printed by Grosvenor Group, Loughton, Essex

CONTENTS

Acknowledgement

The two essays in this publication were given at the Notre Dame Center for Liturgy, Notre Dame University, Indiana, in March 2006. They were later published in two issues of the Center's journal, *Assembly*, Volume 33, Numbers 5 & 6, September 2007. We are grateful to the Center for permission to reprint them.

A Note on the Cover Image

The Luttrell Psalter, from which the cover image is taken, is an illuminated psalter commissioned by Sir Geoffrey Luttrell, lord of the manor of Irnham in Lincolnshire, for his private use. It was written and illustrated on parchment *c.*1320–1340 by anonymous scribes and artists in the diocese of Lincoln.

The illuminated capital B begins the first word of Psalm 1, 'Beatus vir'. King David, who by tradition composed the psalms, is here depicted as young and royal, seated, playing a harp in the style of the fourteenth century to accompany the psalms.

Part One

THE PRAYER OF THE MONKS

THE SECOND LETTER OF PAUL to the Thessalonians contains the injunction which Christians have seen as central to life in Christ, to 'pray without ceasing' (I Thess. 5:17); though how they have practised unceasing prayer has varied. The phrase implies that for all Christians the way of life must also be the way of prayer, so there will always be interplay between life and prayer. It is their lifestyle that makes the difference between those who live as monks and those who do not. Monks are not more responsible for praying than other people. Nor are monks remarkably good, or clever, or well-behaved—some are, some aren't. What they have in common with all humanity is the conviction of their need of mercy; the patron saint of those who pray is, after all, St Mary Magdalene, who was a great sinner (Luke 7:37). In this they are one with all people. Monks, like the majority of humans, are not saints and they are also not clerics; they are essentially laypeople. What makes their way of life different from the average layperson's is their choice to respond to a call of God to remain celibate for the whole of their lives, without dependents, without need for a wage, and with the whole day, especially the night, always free for prayer. Their times for prayer are made possible by their way of life. But the content of their corporate prayer reflects at once their union with all humanity, as creatures before the Creator, as sinners before the Saviour, when they begin their Offices with, 'O God make speed to save me' (Ps. 61:1).

With this in mind, I would like to look at the theme of monastic prayer and its connection with those who are not

1

monks. I will not consider the written details of monastic corporate prayer, but try to see what that prayer was like for the monk and what it meant in his life, noting how the specialised prayer of the monks has always been related to non-monastic Christian living. My sources therefore will not be the usual books of Offices, details of which have been admirably analysed and presented elsewhere,[1] but texts about monks themselves from various sources. I will be referring to the earliest monks in the deserts of Egypt in the fourth century, to monastic prayer in Anglo-Saxon England, and to corporate prayer in the Benedictine and Cistercian traditions.

The main pattern for monastic corporate prayer which has emerged in Western Europe gives a structure to the whole twenty-four hours: Vigils at night, Lauds in the morning, Prime, Terce, Sext, None at intervals during the day, Vespers in the evening and Compline as the last prayer of the day. Within this structure of times of prayer, the material most used in the West has always been the psalter. Since the fifth century, the psalms have been divided between these times of corporate prayer so that the whole psalter is recited every week. There is colour added by the feasts of the saints, the calendar for the year, hymns and scripture readings and readings from the Fathers and from saints' lives; but essentially this monastic corporate prayer is the prayer of the psalms, which are repeated one after another.

Monks can do this because they have chosen to respond to a particular call from God; in practical ways in their use of time they are following a path different from the rest of the baptised. But monks have never had a monopoly on the psalms. In a

---

[1] An excellent discussion of the details of the history of the prayer of the Hours will be found in Paul Bradshaw's writings, particularly in *Two Ways of Praying*, SPCK, 1969.

sense it was the other way round. From the earliest Christian times, the psalms were used in public non-monastic corporate worship, and as such they provided the basis of prayer for all. This practice was naturally taken up and flourished when some of those Christians lived in monasteries or hermitages. In a lively sermon, John Chrysostom (347–407) recommended the psalms for all times and occasions, with a refrain of 'first, last and central is David':

> If we keep vigil in the church, David comes first, last and central. If early in the morning we chant songs and hymns, first, last and central is David again. If we are occupied with the funeral solemnities of those who have fallen asleep, David is first, last and central.

Not only in the solemn liturgies of the great church, he says, but in all gatherings of Christians, learned or not, the psalter is central:

> O amazing wonder! Many who have made little progress in literature know the psalter by heart. Nor is it only in cities and churches that David is famous. In the village market, in the desert, in uninhabitable land or if girls sit at home and spin, he excites the praises of God.

Clearly, John Chrysostom is talking about all the people of God in their ordinary way of life, not the specialist group of monks, for he then goes on to mention them as a kind of epitome of all:

> In monasteries, among those holy choirs of angelic armies, David is first, last and central. In convents of virgins, where are the communities of those who imitate Mary, in deserts where there are men crucified to the world, who live their life in heaven with God, David is first, last and central. All other men at night are asleep, David alone is active, and gathering the saints of God

into seraphic bands, he turns earth into heaven and converts men into angels. [2]

Conversion for all is the basic theme of the use of the psalms here. Augustine of Hippo (c.354–430) also commended the psalms to his secular congregation in a series of amazing sermons based on them, which are seen as essential to all life in Christ, not just as an end in themselves. He stressed the inner meaning of this recitation of psalms as an image of the crucified Christian life in his sermon on verse 4 of Psalm 149, 'Let them praise his name in chorus on timbrel and psaltery:'

> On the timbrel leather is stretched, on the psaltery leather is stretched, on either instrument the flesh is crucified. How well did he 'sing a psalm on timbrel and psaltery' who said, 'the world is crucified to me and I unto the world' (Gal. 6:14). This psaltery or timbrel He wishes thee to take up, who loveth a new song who teacheth thee, saying to thee, 'whosoever will be my disciple, let him deny himself and take up his cross and follow me' (Matt. 16:24). Let him not set down his psaltery, let him not set down his timbrel, let him stretch himself out on the wood and be dried from the lust of the flesh. The more the strings are stretched, the more sharply they sound. The apostle Paul, then, in order that his psaltery might sound sharply, what said he? 'Stretching forth for those things that are before,' etc. (Phil. 3:13). He stretched himself; Christ touched him; and the sweetness of truth sounded. [3]

---

[2] John Chrysostom, 'Panegyric on the Psalter', in *The Holy Psalter*, ed. E. Moore, Madras 1966, p. xxv.

[3] St Augustine, *Expositions on the Book of Psalms,* trans. A. Cleveland Coxe, Nicene and Post Nicene Fathers, Vol. VIII, Eerdmans, reprinted 1979, p. 678.

This kind of prayer for all the baptised points to the psalms as a basic link between monastic and non-monastic prayer. The psalter was most easily learned by heart when said one psalm after another; it could thus become an integral part of the one knowing it. An early writer said of the Egyptian monks, 'They meditate the psalter by heart when they are on their own'. This is the main contribution of the Desert Fathers to later liturgy: they learnt to say the psalter by heart and they said it continuously, one psalm after another. There is no point in saying the psalter continuously if you are not going to be there for the next bit; it presumes a stable lifestyle. Some of the monks chose to say the whole psalter privately also, all of it in a day, sometimes two psalters in a day, and that is a theme which continued later.

The man who conveyed the tradition of the desert to the emerging monasticism of Gaul was John Cassian, most of all in his *Institutes*.[4] Remembering the Thebaid, he described the corporate Office of the Desert Fathers and said that the number of psalms was fixed at twelve for the evening Office and for the Office at night. 'This arrangement,' he says, 'was fixed long ago and has continued unbroken to the present day in all monasteries in Egypt.'[5] The psalms were a structure for prayer but it was not quantity that mattered. The psalms were never the end, as Augustine most clearly showed. They were a way into full life in Christ. The psalms were essential in the corporate and personal prayer of the monks but they opened out, blossoming into the fullness of Christian prayer. This sense of the psalms as a gateway into conversion of heart is made clear in this story told about the early monks:

---

[4] John Cassian, *Institutes,* trans E. L. S. Gibson, Nicene and Post-Nicene Fathers, Series 2, Michigan (reprint) 1973,Vol. XI, pp. 205–218.
[5] Ibid.

The blessed Epiphanius, Bishop of Cyprus, was told this by the abbot of a monastery which he visited in Palestine: 'We do not neglect our appointed round of psalmody, but we are very careful to recite Terce, Sext and None'. Then Epiphanius corrected them with the following comment: 'It is clear that you do not trouble about the other hours of the day if you cease from prayer. The true monk should have prayer and psalmody continually in his heart'.[6]

Epiphanius was indicating the place of the corporate times of prayer in the whole life of conversion; the round of corporate psalmody, Terce, Sext and None, was seen as a minimum, a structure in time, to be built on. What lay beyond this minimum for the monks of the desert?

A young monk, Lot, went to a more experienced monk, Joseph and said to him: 'As far as I can I say my little Office, I fast a little, I pray and meditate, I live in peace as far as I can, I purify my thoughts. What else can I do?' The hermit stood up and stretched his hands towards heaven. His fingers became like ten lamps of fire, and he said to him: 'If you will, you can become all flame'.[7]

The maximum of the desert was the total life consumed by the fire of the Holy Spirit. This contrast comes out again and again in these texts. John Cassian saw the daily structure of monastic prayer as basic; but beyond that there was 'the prayer of fire'.

The prayer of the monk depended on the continuous recitation of the psalter and listening to the reading of the rest of the Bible not selected but in sequence. This was the structure

---

[6] *Sayings of the Desert Fathers*, trans. Benedicta Ward SLG, Mowbray/Cistercian Studies, 1975, Epiphanius 3, p. 48–9. Hereinafter *Sayings*.
[7] *Sayings*, Joseph of Panephysis 7, p. 88.

but not the end. For instance, *The Life of St. Daniel the Stylite* reports that after he had lived for some time in the monastery and followed the normal discipline, his disciple Sergius had a dream in which three angels ordered him to tell Daniel that

> the appointed time of thy discipline in this church [i.e. the monastery] is now fulfilled, from henceforth leave the church, come hither and begin thy contest.[8]

Daniel was being told to begin the 'real' life of prayer, to leave the place where he had been formed in the disciplines of praying the psalms, with the structure already established in him, and to stand for the rest of his life on a column outside Constantinople as a visible sign of mediation between earth and heaven.

When considering this ceaseless psalmody of the desert, it is notable that most of the monks were illiterate men who knew things not by reading but by hearing and memorising them. They had memories that really worked and they knew the psalter by heart; therefore they could pray in the night just as well as in the daytime. Night prayer was of special value to the monks and they were concerned to use it well. What they discussed in Scetis was not whether they should pray for one hour during the night but whether they should allow themselves to sleep for one hour during the night. Arsenius said: 'One hour of sleep is enough for a monk'.[9] Pachomius stood all night in prayer for several nights. The official Vigils in the desert are the well-known ones of Saturday to Sunday, particularly in Nitria where the monks met together for the weekly gathering for public worship, the Synaxis, before dawn on Sundays, but this

---

[8] *Life of Daniel the Stylite,* in *Three Byzantine Saints,* trans. Elizabeth Dawes and Norman Baynes, Mowbray 1948, ch. 23, p. 20.
[9] *Sayings,* Arsenius 15, p. 9.

was never enough. There was in Egypt a tradition of the 'Sleepless Ones' and one of the monasteries had that title. Rufinus, visiting the desert at the end of the fourth century, says that they did not lie down to sleep at night, but if they had to fall asleep they did so standing or sitting. They simply snatched sleep, thinking only of continually being alert for prayer.[10]

But the mark of all the monks, not just the non-sleeping ones, was continual prayer and psalmody, alone or together. The same author says,

> We came to Nitria, the best known of all; in this place there are fifty dwellings. They are divided by their dwellings, but they remain bound in faith and love.[11]

Rufinus wrote this remembering how he and his companions arrived there and the monks came out to meet them. He goes on to say that the first thing they did was to say psalms with the monks in their corporate prayer. Even among the extreme hermits there was a pattern of meeting for the corporate prayer of the psalms in the night between Saturday and Sunday. He describes Cellia, the extreme desert to which those who had been initiated into the life of prayer and wanted to live more remotely, withdrew:

> This is utter desert; the cells are divided from each other so that no one can hear the voice of his neighbour; there is a great silence and a huge quiet. Only on Saturday and Sunday do they meet in church and then they see each other face to face as men restored to heaven.[12]

---

[10] Rufinus, *Lives of the Desert Fathers*, trans. Norman Russell, Preface by Benedicta Ward SLG, Mowbray and Cistercian Studies 1980, p. 148. Hereinafter *Lives*.
[11] Ibid.
[12] Ibid.

Here again the rule of the monks is that they *want* to pray the psalms and watch as much as they possibly can to become filled with the life of God. Abbot Poemen was asked: 'Father, what do you do if a young monk falls asleep during Vigils?' He answered: 'I take his head upon my knee and help him to sleep more comfortably.'[13] The assumption of the monks is that everyone wants to be awake, that wakefulness at Vigils is something to be desired and if someone cannot manage to do so, it is not because of idleness but out of genuine fatigue. Later monks also kept to this tradition, like John, prior of Clairvaux who thought up a device for keeping himself on the watch constantly:

> Above his stall he put an ingenious mechanism and if by chance he began to close his eyes because of the fatigue of vigils, his head would nod against a hammer which would come down and by its blow would suddenly help him not to fall asleep.[14]

With oneself, one was always rigorous; with others, one was always compassionate, if the life beneath the psalms had begun to do its work in the soul. The recitation of the psalms was the entry into heaven and therefore part of a whole life; it engendered not grudging acquiescence but delight. In Egypt, Apollo said that nobody in his monastery was allowed to be gloomy or downcast. They were always to be giving thanks: 'Rejoicing always, praying without ceasing and giving thanks in everything',[15] echoing the verse in Thessalonians that comes before 'Pray without ceasing,' which is, 'Rejoice evermore.' It

---

[13] *Sayings*, Poemen 92, p. 151.
[14] Conrad of Eberbach, *The Great Beginning of Cîteaux*, trans. Benedicta Ward SLG and Paul Savage, Cistercian Publications/ Liturgical Press 2012, p. 334. Hereinafter *Conrad*.
[15] *Lives*, Apollo, p. 70.

was unbecoming for monks to look miserable, and their long vigils were to result in joy. The tradition of love and joy in the psalms continued and is found again in many places. For instance, in the eleventh century Anselm wrote to the depressed and grumbling monk Helinand, that monastic life might seem like an insupportable weight but it was a weight to be borne singing.[16]

This free choice of corporate and private daily prayer of the psalms by the monks was integral to their life, and their delight in it was hard-won; it could indeed be *pondus insupportabilis*. No serious person supposes that living any form of Christian life is easy. In or out of a monastery there is the same inner spiritual contest to be undergone. The idea of a neat orderly line of simple chanting monks who easily enjoy what they are doing is a myth. Choir was an arena, an open space for the work done by God in each. And that meant combat with the demons as well as the witness of the angels. There are innumerable stories about the angels and the demons of the monastic choir, beginning with Egypt, and one of the great monks, Macarius:

> One night the devil came and knocked on the door of his cell and said, 'Get up, Macarius, and go to the meeting, where the brethren have met to celebrate vigils.' Macarius, said: 'You liar and enemy of the truth, what do you know about the meeting, when we are gathered together with the saints?' The demon replied: 'Don't you realise that there is never any meeting or gathering of the monks for prayer without us?' So Macarius went and found the brothers had met to celebrate vigils … and behold he saw the whole church filled with monks

---

[16] *Letters of St Anselm of Canterbury*, trans. Walter Frohlich, Kalamazoo, Michigan, 1990, Vol. I, Letter 121 'To Helinand', p. 252.

who were praying. It was also filled with little black Ethiopian boys who ran among them.[17]

Macarius watched them very carefully. He saw all the brothers being tempted in different ways and when they come out of church Macarius asked each one, 'What were you thinking about during the Vigils?' His interest, in fact, was not in the celebration of the rite but in the interior prayer of the heart. What mattered was individual purification of mind, not the way a thing is done, but why it is undertaken. The Office was but a part of a whole life of asceticism by which the monk was becoming more ready to listen to God.

This theme of the Office as a place of celestial warfare continued in the West. For instance, Peter Damian, a hermit in Italy in the eleventh century, wrote a 'Treatise on the bell-ringer who summons the brethren to Office', and used the same kind of military images about the Office of the monks:

We march out to battle like a camp, we hasten to the church to pray and sing the Office, for there the princes of darkness wage deadly war against us, so that by distracting our minds with fantastic thoughts they may turn us from the words our lips are uttering. But indeed what a splendid army it is, especially at night, when the brethren aroused as if by the sound of a trumpet, form a wedge and march like an ordered battle column. They come forth inspired and ready for action in battle on the Lord's behalf.[18]

The idea of the choir as a place of combat, as the arena for the fight with the interior demons is here again emphasised.

---

[17] *Lives*, Macarius of Alexandria, p. 153.
[18] Peter Damian, 'On the Perfection of Monks', trans. Patricia McNulty, in *St Peter Damian*, Faber and Faber, 1959, ch. 17, pp. 117–118.

Stories about the presence of angels and demons during corporate prayer continued in these later sources. The Cistercian, Conrad of Eberbach, wrote in the thirteenth century that in the Office:

> The Lord does not consider quantity of material but affection of heart in the sacrifices of piety offered him, and let them remember that it is all nothing unless they are entirely consumed by the flame of devotion.[19]

He illustrated this by the following story:

> There was a monk who had a magnificent natural voice. He used to stand as if dumb and outside the psalmody while the brothers sang in praise of God. But when it came to the verse of the responds for which he was responsible, he sang in his usual worldly way, with a strong and sharp vocal clarity, with grace notes and vibrato, and without any of the gravity that is suitable in the praise of God. When it was over, in order that he and the others standing around might understand the result of such a ridiculous performance, there appeared to their sight a devil in the form of a little Ethiopian boy, hideous and black, who clapped his impure hands and cried in a strange raucous tone, 'Bravo, bravo, O well sung; that was excellent!'[20]

This rebuke to the pride of the young singer was no doubt all the more galling for him since the other brothers heard the praise of the demon. This story is paralleled in the same source by a story of an angel who was seen to take care of an old and sick monk in choir:

---

[19] *Conrad*, p. 442.
[20] Idem p. 456–7.

Arnulf, a rich convert of Bernard and a monk of Clairvaux, was so weak and broken by suffering that he could only bow with the greatest difficulty in choir. But he would not omit this and bowed deeply and reverently every time the 'Glory be to the Father' was sung. When he was present one day at Vespers in the church, in the rear choir, there was an equally devout monk beside him. This man saw an angel of the Lord appear in the form of a very handsome young man, in a habit white as snow, but Arnulf did not see him. When the Gloria was sung in the psalm, and Arnulf bowed as was his custom, the angel of the Lord who was beside him supported his head. When the monk next to Arnulf saw this, and realised from the brightness of his face and clothing that it was an angel, he was overjoyed and went up to him to take hold of him and embrace him. But when he held out his hands to touch him, the angel suddenly was not there, but appeared again in another place. The monk saw him and ran after him and tried to hold him again, but the angel vanished again, and each time the monk tried to catch him it was in vain. At last the angel vanished completely, letting the monk see him but not laying hold of him.[21]

The angel was not seen by the sick monk but by another, who found himself jealous; no doubt the demons were also at work here. This picture of angelic hide-and-seek in a monastic choir incidentally suggests a less than formal situation there.

With this concentration on the psalter in corporate and individual prayer in the West, what place was held by intellectual understanding of the psalms? Always surrounded by the

---

[21] Idem p. 458.

'converting ordinance' of psalmody, were the monks also concerned with academic understanding of the psalter? Some monks would have a fine intellectual and biblical education and be concerned with the grammatical meaning of the words of the psalms. This was shown above all in the Christological interpretation they gave to the psalter. In saying the psalms, the bread of the word of God was broken and eaten. There was little inclination to alter the actual words of translations of psalms since these were seen as a sacrament of the word of God to the participants, though there are a few instances of some such changes. What was important was that the texts of the psalms should be absorbed into the heart, since they were seen as more than human words, for in them God spoke through David as a prophet of Christ.

In various ways the Office indicated to believers that the psalms were illuminated by the light of Christ falling upon their pages. The psalms were the words of Christ to the Father, and they became the prayer of the monk insofar as he was in Christ. To articulate this sense, the addition of other words could interpret a psalm. The simplest was the conclusion of each psalm with the words, 'Glory be to Father, and to the Son, and to the Holy Spirit,' directing the prayer of the psalm to the Trinity. Antiphons were used to bring out the Christological meaning of each psalm in its context, that is, phrases were sung either before or during the chanting of the psalm, indicating its inner meaning. Psalter collects also interpreted the words of each psalm. These were prayers read at the conclusion of a psalm or group of psalms to direct prayer towards Christ.[22] Sometime the Little Hours were linked with the moments of the Passion of Christ through the day. There are examples, for

---

[22] Cf. *The Psalter Collects from V–VIth Century Sources* (Three Series) André Wilmart & Louis Brou, Henry Bradshaw Society 1949, Vol. 83, p. xxv.

instance in the Utrecht psalter and its companions, where there is a detailed drawing before each psalm, giving Christological meaning to it.[23]

The importance of the Christological understanding of the psalms of the Office can be seen in this example from Anglo-Saxon England in the seventh century in the monastery of St Paul at Jarrow after the plague of 686:

> In the monastery over which Ceolfrith presided all those brethren who could read or preach or recite the antiphons and responds were taken away, with the exception of the abbot and one little lad who had been reared and taught by him, and who is at this time still in the same monastery where he holds the rank of priest, and both by written and spoken words justly commends his teacher's praiseworthy acts to all who desire to know of them. Now he (I mean the abbot) being much distressed by reason of the aforesaid pestilence, gave command that, their former use being suspended, they should go through the whole psalter, except at Matins and Vespers, without the recitation of the antiphons. And when this practise had been followed, not without many tears and lamentation on his part, for the space of one week, being unable to endure it any longer he resolved once again that the customary order of the psalms with their antiphons should be restored.[24]

'Tears' and 'lamentation' indicate considerable distress and I do not suppose that Ceolfrith was so upset at having had to omit the antiphons simply because the Offices sounded more

---

[23] There are many excellent modern editions of these texts, e.g., *The Eadwine Psalter*, eds Margaret Gibson, Richard W. Pfaff & T. A. Heslop, London and Pennsylvania, 1992.

[24] *Life of St Ceolfrith*, trans. D. S. Boutflower, London, 1912, ch. 4, p. 65.

impressive when sung in full, nor out of a legalistic sense that everything must be included. It was, after all, perfectly acceptable to simplify the Office in this way and such a practice was recommended in the *Rule of St Benedict* The words of this account convey a sense of intolerable loss which surely must have come from the absence of the antiphons whose words made the psalms into Christian prayers. Ceolfrith's devotion to the psalter was outstanding even for his own times. At Jarrow, he recited the psalter twice daily in addition to the Offices, and on his last journey to Rome, he daily chanted the psalter of David in order three times over. For him the psalms were the basic scaffolding for all his prayer as a Christian.

But as well as this concentration on the Christological meaning of the psalms of the Offices, was there also an intellectual examination of these psalm texts? In the deserts of Egypt, there was great caution about intellectual work in case it led to pride. There was this notable dialogue about it:

> The brethren said, 'By what means did the fathers sing the psalms of the Holy Spirit without distraction?' The old man said, 'First of all they accustomed themselves whenever they stood up to sing the service in their cells, to work carefully at collecting their attention and understanding to the meaning of the psalms, and they took care never to let a word escape them without knowing its meaning, not as a mere matter of history, like the interpreters, nor after the manner of the translator like Basil or John Chrysostom, but spiritually, according to the interpretation of the fathers; that is to say, they applied all the psalms to their own lives and

works and to their passions and to their inner life and to the war that the devil waged against them.[25]

This was a tradition that continued. For instance, in the eleventh century in England, Christina of Markyate, whose name is connected with the beautifully illustrated St Alban's psalter, was concerned only with the spiritual meaning of the psalms, known by heart and accepted and with *sapientia*, the wisdom that knows by participating. Her advice to a monk was that the psalter should be known by heart, so that

> your heart's desire is your prayer; if your desire continues uninterrupted, so does your prayer. Inward prayer without ceasing is the desire of the heart. Whatever else you are doing, if you continue to doing it for God you do not cease to pray.[26]

She selected just the verses that expressed and strengthened her own desire for God. In the same way, the mystics such as Mechtild of Hackeborn and Elisabeth of Schönau linked their visions with the psalter and the Office. The psalter was to be chanted and meaning would be revealed through it. But this was not the only approach. Héloïse, Christina's exact contemporary, took a different line, for Abelard advised her and her community to use the psalms with intelligence. Héloïse herself was not ready to absorb the inner meaning of the psalms unless the external words were right, an approach she says she had seen in Augustine's *De Genesis ad Literam*. She wrote to Abelard:

> We are still uncertain who is the author of the translation of the psalter which the Gallican church uses. If we want to judge from the sayings of those who have

---

[25] *The Paradise of the Holy Fathers*, trans. E. A. W. Budge, London, 1907, Vol. II, p. 306.
[26] *Life of Christina of Markyate*, ed. and trans. C. H. Talbot, Oxford, 1959, p. 101.

exposed the diversity of translations, it departs from the universal interpretation and carries no weight of authority, as I think. Indeed, long habit of tradition has prevailed in this, so that while with other texts we have copies corrected by the blessed Jerome, with the psalter which we use a great deal we are following what is inauthentic.[27]

Abelard replied:

I hasten to send you the psalter which you had earnestly begged from me so that you may offer a perpetual sacrifice of prayer to the Lord for our many and great offences ... for the food of the soul and its spiritual refreshment is the God-given understanding of scripture.[28]

Moreover, the meditation of the psalter chanted in Vigils provided the right setting for at least one philosophical insight — and that the greatest of the Middle Ages—Anselm's formulation of the Ontological Argument for the existence of God:

Suddenly one night during Matins (*inter nocturnas vigilias*) the grace of God illuminated his heart, the whole matter became clear to his mind, and a great joy and exultation filled his whole being. Thinking therefore that others would be glad to know what he had found, he immediately (*ilico*—on the spot) and ungrudgingly (*livore carens*) wrote it on writing tablets and gave them to one of the brethren of the monastery for safe keeping.[29]

---

[27] Abelard, *Hymnarius*, Book 1, Preface, Migne *PL* 178, col. 1771. Cf. *Letters of Abelard and Heloise*, trans. B. Radice, Penguin Classics, Harmondsworth 1974, re-edited M. Clancy, 2003, Letter 8, p. 164.

[28] Abelard, *Petri Abelardi Opera Theologica V; Expositio in Hexameron*, ed. Mary Romig, Preface, David Luscombe, CCCM 15, Turnhout 2004, p. 4.

[29] Eadmer *Life of St. Anselm*, ed. and trans. R. W. Southern, Oxford 1962, p. 30.

Anselm later placed the argument within the long prayer of the *Proslogion*: he had received it in choir, a place of inspiration within a known frame-work, where the mind was at rest and open to God and therefore to inspiration. Here intellect and heart were united in hearing the word of God.

Increasingly in the later Middle Ages, people were also trained academics before they became monks, so that there was an increase in discussion of the text of the psalms. Mainly, however, it was the inner understanding of the psalter as the work of God within the soul that mattered to monks. Monks were formed by the psalter and it is noteworthy that many of them died repeating the words of the psalms. When Bede was dying, his constant companion, the monk Cuthbert, noted that he 'spent the rest of the day chanting the psalter as best he could.'[30] Other saints have also died with the psalms as the basis of their prayer. For instance, in the fourth century Augustine had the seven Penitential Psalms always before him, and Teresa of Avila in the sixteenth repeated over and over again the verse from Psalm 51, 'a broken and a contrite heart, O God, thou wilt not despise'.

---

[30] Bede, *Ecclesiastical History of the English People*, ed. and trans. B. Colgrave and R. A. B Mynors, Oxford 1969, 'Letter of Cuthbert on the Death of Bede', pp. 581–587. Hereinafter *EHEP*.

Part Two

THE INNER PRAYER OF THE PSALTER FOR ALL

HOW WERE these psalms and canticles sung? Presumably, with one or more voices of trained cantors for the psalms, with the repetitive sentences of antiphons as a chorus, either at the beginning and end or repeated after each or several verses. Aethelwulf, describing the chanting in a cell of the monastery of Lindisfarne in the eighth century, says of Siwine, the fifth abbot, that

> when the reverend festivals of God's saints came round and when between two choirs in the church he sang the verses of the psalms among the brothers they rendered in song the sweet sounding music of the flowing antiphon; and the lector, a man very learned in books, poured forth song to the general delight, singing in a clear voice.[31]

When Augustine came to Kent, he and his companions met in the church of St Martin to 'chant the psalms, first and then to pray, to say mass, to preach and to baptise.'[32] Aidan and his companions occupied themselves either with 'reading the scriptures or learning the psalms'[33]. It is no wonder that Bede, their historian and heir, placed the psalms at the heart of his life in 'the daily task (*cura*) of singing in the church,'[34] which he described as his delight. Elsewhere he wrote:

---

[31] Aethelwulf, *De Abbatibus*, ed. A. Campbell, Oxford 1967, ch. 15, p. 40.
[32] Bede *EHEP*, Book I, p. 75.
[33] Idem Book III, p. 227.
[34] Idem Book V, p. 567.

We traditionally spend the night vigil joyfully singing additional psalms and hearing a larger number of lessons, in a church where many lights are burning and the walls are adorned more lavishly than usual.[35]

Here as elsewhere there was emphasis on music, on chanting the psalms. The use of plain chant, that is, all voices united on one note, was both useful as a technique and meaningful about the unity of a community. Coming out of a culture where all reading was audible, the saying of the Offices was necessarily vocal, even when a monk was alone, demanding the participation of the body as well as the mind.

This inner understanding of the *Opus Dei* as the work God does in each one was basic for the monastic office. But the monks of the west were surrounded and indeed supported by non-monks, especially patronised by great lords. What use was the stable chanting of psalms to them? The fact that the prayer of the monks was always there, always available, always visibly present, was appreciated but it was not enough; those outside wanted to be more included, and the influence of their expectations on the Office was considerable. The psalm-prayers of the monks at the Office soon included extra prayers, extra psalms, especially for rulers and benefactors. The meditation of the corporate Office of the monks was gradually being transformed into vocal prayer for specific people and causes.

It is a commonplace to say that monastic prayer, focused in corporate meetings by day and night, was part of the prayer of Christ for the world. There would be no point in it otherwise. But the outsiders brought a more specific view in which the

---

[35] *Sermons of the Venerable Bede*, 'Sermon for the Dedication of a Church,' Homily Book 2:25, ed. D. Hurst & J. Fraipont, CCSL 122, Turnhout 1955, p. 368.

monks were seen as praying not *with* all but *instead of* all. From the fourth century onwards the monks had been seen by the outsiders as angels—angels on earth who are praying before God and already a part of the angelic choir. The monastery was the gate of heaven. This pressure of definition put upon monks by the outside world can be traced back to the desert. It is there in the *History of the Monks in Egypt* written in the first century of Egyptian monasticism.[36] Seven tourists-monks went to Egypt from Palestine in 394. They made their way down the Nile, visited the hermits and the monasteries, and afterwards one of them wrote a diary in which there are the observations of a monk but of an outsider to the desert, one who did not belong to that particular pattern of monastic life. He wrote a eulogy about how wonderful the monks were: 'I saw new prophets who had attained a God-like state'. 'One can see them scattered in the desert waiting for Christ like loyal sons watching for their father, or like an army expecting its emperor, or like a sober household looking forward to the arrival of its master and liberator.' There is here the familiar theme of the expectation of the coming of the kingdom, the eschatological aspect of monastic life with which the monks would have agreed. 'There is only the expectation of the coming of Christ in the singing of hymns.' But then he goes on to say: 'It is clear to all who dwell there (he means those not in monasteries) that through them the world is kept in being, and that through them, too, human life is preserved and honoured by God.' When they got to Scetis, he says:

> I also saw another vast company of monks of all ages living in the desert and in the countryside. Their number is past counting. There are so many of them that an

---

[36] *Lives*, Prologue, pp. 49–51.

earthly emperor could not assemble so large an army. For there is no town or village in Egypt and the Thebaid which is not surrounded by monasteries as if by walls. And the people depend on the prayers of the monks as if on God himself.[37]

'Those through whom the world is kept in being.' This is an outsider's definition. It is what others say about the monks; it is never used by the monks of themselves. Nearer to it is the story of Palladius who, getting thoroughly bored with the life and prayer of the desert, said to Macarius: 'The devils of boredom are tempting me to leave'. Macarius replied: Tell them 'that for Christ's sake I am guarding the walls.'[38] A monk can say this to remind himself to carry on with what he is doing, but he cannot make it the definition of his life. The problem lies in what is done to the monks by others. The monks are given this place as the ones who pray for the world, the ones through whom the world is kept in being.

This external definition of the place of the monk in society took a definite form during the Middle Ages and this had its effect on their corporate prayer. Here is an instance of how prayers around the Office increased under pressure from out-side. The *Regularis Concordia*,[39] drawn up by Dunstan in the tenth century in England, is almost entirely concerned with details of liturgy, the Office and the Mass. It no longer pre-sented a balanced round of work and psalmody, but a complete life of liturgical devotion, a continual meeting for the worship of God and visible, audible intercession for the world. Great care was taken to see that the details were right and seen to be right. The monk was seen as belonging to a class whose job it is

[37] *Lives*, Prologue 10, p. 50.
[38] Palladius, *Lausiac History*, trans. R. T. Meyer, London, 1965, p. 67.
[39] *Regularis Concordia*, ed. and trans. Thomas Symonds, Oxford, 1953.

to pray, particularly to pray for society, to pray for others. It was no longer the ascetic discipline of the individual that came first. The Preface to the *Regularis Concordia* explains the understanding its creator had of the Office. King Edgar and his wife, who with Dunstan called the Council at Winchester, stated in their Preface that the canons who had been performing the Office in the cathedrals were 'almost wholly lacking in the service of our Lord. So we will place in their stead, for the service of God, monks and nuns.'[40] The monks and nuns were to be experts in public prayer, but how they prayed was still connected with how they lived. Edgar urged them to be of one mind; their customs had to tend to 'uprightness of life and regular discipline'. They were to be 'watchful for good works' and 'they must pray for the King and their benefactors that they may receive the reward of eternal life'.

The monks were to see corporate prayer as their first task and add on prayers for others. This meant that the monks were required to get up extra early for Night Office and a lot of prayers had to be said before getting even as far as Matins. Fifteen psalms had to be recited—presumably the Gradual Psalms—and later the Penitential Psalms as well. After each Hour there were prayers for benefactors and friends, and penitential psalms for the dead. A litany was said daily after Prime, again for benefactors. The Office of All Souls was invented at Cluny, and after each Office there was not only the Office of the Dead but also the Office of All Saints; later the Office of the Virgin was added. The Office had to be visible, the monks had to be seen doing it, and their life-style had to conform to this promise. They became in fact living prayer-wheels, or like the Beaver in the *Hunting of the Snark:*

---

[40] Idem pp. 1–2.

There was also a beaver, that paced on the deck,
    Or would sit making lace in the bow:
And had often (the Bellman said) saved them from wreck,
    Though none of the sailors knew how.[41]

Another influence tending to increase the amount of corporate vocal prayer in choir was the desire of non-monks to be associated legally with monks, as 'confrères' and so the confraternities came into being. At Newminster, for instance, the confrères numbered about two thousand and a commemoration of them by name was made daily in the Office. At Canterbury the confrères were urged to share in Mass, Matins, Vigils and other prayers, as well as in fasting and alms, and other good works whenever possible. This was not a casual association but one in which non-monks were counted in some sense as members of the community, so that burial rights went along with it. In the end, patrons wanted to be buried near the place where the monastic office was said, so that they would be in the right place at the Resurrection:

What shall I, frail man, be pleading?
Who for me be interceding,
When the just are mercy needing?[42]

This external pressure on the monastic Office in the Middle Ages came from a world in which there was a theory of the division of society into those who pray, those who fight and those who work. The monk was increasingly defined as a choir monk, a *monachus chorum*. Another factor must be taken into account; from this time onwards, more and more monks in monasteries were ordained. Conversely, by this time, all clergy were regarded as monks; the distinction between monastic and

---

[41] *The Hunting of the Snark*, Lewis Carroll. First edition Macmillan, 1876.
[42] *Dies Irae*, Thomas of Celano, trans. W. J. Jones, *New English Hymnal* 524.

canonical office became confused to the point of being meaningless. Originally the rules which contained regulations for the monks about the Office were spiritual guides for the individual, tools to be used. The interest was not in uniformity of detail but in the place of the Office in the whole life. However the rules now began to be regarded as judicial codes which in all their details equalled the monastic life. This introduces at least one important question: the phrase *opus Dei*[43] must mean primarily the work God is doing in the soul of the monk who is present. The Office is one of the works of obedience to which nothing else should be preferred. But the phrase was increasingly interpreted as 'work done for God', as a professional activity in the world, to mean, in fact, only the corporate moments of prayer in the monastery.

The influence of the Office is vividly shown in the fact that the monks now created texts for personal use for non-monks, based on the psalms used in the Office. These were Books of Hours, illustrated abbreviations of the monastic office for lay folk to use, often marvellous works of art, making the monastic psalter the basis for private devotion. This was a good expansion of the use of the psalter away from the monastery; in a way it took the psalms back to their earlier use in the market-place. For anyone, to use the words of the psalms to articulate present terror and grief, as well as joy and wonder, is to discover

---

[43] *Opus Dei*: The corporate prayer of the monks is often referred to as *opus Dei*, and translated as 'the work of God'. See an article by I. Hausherr, 'Opus Dei' in *Orientalia Christiana Periodica* 13, 1947, pp. 95–218, for a full discussion of the misunderstanding of the genitive which caused the Office to be thought of a 'the work monks do for God'. This is not its primary meaning; it must mean 'the work God does in us'. The famous phrase, 'Let nothing be put before the work of God,' comes in Section 43 of the Rule when Benedict is talking about the importance of punctuality in relation to obedience, not when he is talking about the Office only, but of the need to be always alert and ready for the work God means for us.

through them hope beyond hope. As a cry of protest against the inhumanity of man the words of the psalms are always especially appropriate. Whether the horror is personal or cosmic, whether it is Christ on the Cross, genocide among nations, exile from a monastic home, the loss of someone held dear, or the personal anguish of the dying, the words of the psalms express that for which we have no words and at the same voice: 'I am so fast in prison that I cannot get out'; 'O deliver me from them that persecute me for they are too strong for me'; 'my God, my God, why hast thou forsaken me?'

This was as true outside as inside the monastery. As a seventh century writer put it:

> If any oppressive sorrow has come upon you, either by an injury brought on by others, or by a besetting fault, or by an overwhelming domestic loss; if you grieve for any reason at all, do not murmur against one another or place the blame on God, but rather pray with psalms to the Lord lest the sadness of the world which is death swallow you up; drive the destructive sickness of grief from your heart by the frequent sweetness of the psalms.[44]

The psalms were a structure for monastic prayer and one monk, Bede, did more than use the psalms in this intensely personal way: he popularised their use outside the cloister by composing a new kind of prayer from them in his Abbreviated Psalter.[45] He selected verses from each psalm which could be

---

[44] Bede, *Commentary on the Seven Catholic Epistles*, trans. D. Hurst, Cistercian Publications, Michigan, 1985. 'Commentary on James 5:13', pp. 199–200.
[45] *Collectio Psalterii Baedae*, ed. J. Fraipont, *Bedae Venerabilis Opera*, CCSL 122, Turnhout, 1955, pp. 452–470. For a translation and full discussion of this text see Benedicta Ward, *Bede and the Psalter* (Jarrow Lecture 1991), SLG Press, Fairacres Publications FP141, 2002, p. xv.

used as direct prayer or praise, as food for meditation, as a plea for mercy, or as protest, or contrition, or as adoration and exultation. Sometimes one verse alone was used, sometimes several. The verses were also selected as a memory device, so that a sense of the meaning of the psalm as whole was retained; it would be possible to recall the whole psalm from these clues. The *Abbreviations from the Psalter* marked a turning point in the history of prayer in the West, providing a popular vehicle for devotion for the next four centuries.

The man who was most enthusiastically vocal in his praise of the psalter as a book for prayer was also an Englishman, also from the north; this was Alcuin, a pupil of the school of Egbert, Bede's colleague at York. Alcuin recommended the psalter earnestly as the basis of intimate prayer, speaking out of the same monastic tradition of compunction as Bede, but carrying it into another level of self-awareness. Alcuin had more interest in the interior needs of the praying person. The words of the psalm were seen as the perfect expression of human praise, wonder, love, and delight as well as sorrow, repentance and sometimes of revolt and protest, though with a strong sense of the external form of the psalms. In this he belongs to the monastic world, especially to the tradition of the solitary life, and he expanded and elaborated the way indicated by Bede when he wrote:

> In the psalms, if you look carefully, you will find an intimacy of prayer such as you could never discover by yourself. In the psalms you will find an intimate confession of your sins, and a perfect supplication for divine mercy. In the psalms you will find an intimate thanksgiving for all that befalls you. In the psalms you confess your weakness and misery and thereby call down God's mercy upon you. You will find every virtue

in the psalms if you are worthy of God's mercy in deigning to reveal to you their secrets.[46]

Where Bede had provided, and Alcuin recommended, a selection from the psalms which preserved the shape of the psalm but made it available for personal prayer, a Carolingian writer, copying the form, created a different and even more popular Abbreviated Psalter. Where Bede had begun from the psalter text, the new compiler began from the needs of the individual for prayers. Taking the great themes of compunction, repentance and thanksgiving, he selected only those verses from the psalter that expressed those ideas in the first person. Not every psalm therefore was represented, and the verses were no longer a key to the full version of the psalm. The change to the use of only those phrases which expressed emotion was to be even more far-reaching. Men of a solitary habit of prayer continued to make their own extracts along these lines; increasingly the starting point was not the given words of David but the personal need and desires of the one praying. The hermit saint Anchaire (AD 865), for instance, did this:

> from the passages of the Bible which led to compunction
> he made for himself out of each psalm a little prayer. ...
> He was hardly concerned at all with the order of the
> words; he sought only compunction of heart.[47]

The tradition of the abbreviated psalter was based on the monastic Office, and began as a memory-device, a reminder of the whole psalm. Also through the selected verses the heart could pray and direct itself to God in a way contained within the scriptures. It was ideally suited to provide a structure for prayer for non-monastic persons concerned with the prayer of

---

[46] Alcuin, *De Psalmorum Usu*, Preface, Migne, *PL* 101 col. 465.
[47] St Rembert, *Life of St. Anchaire*, Migne, *PL* 118, col. 1000.

29

the heart. But it did not remain the possession of the few. A note added to a Durham copy of the Abbreviated Psalter suggests that it should be used by laymen who:

> have worldly business, who lie in sickness, who undertake long journeys, sail in ships or go to war; they sing this psalter assiduously and they gain thereby the heavenly kingdom.

It was a return to the use of the psalms in the early church described by Chrysostom and Augustine.

The Abbreviated Psalter, in its *verba mea* form, contained within it the basis for the prayer of the heart for the Middle Ages, outside as well as inside the monasteries. It had a central place in the articulation of devotion, until a new age found another channel for that same compunction of heart in lengthy meditations which provided other words for the same kind of prayer.

This personal and interior prayer was a strong current flowering in a great tradition. When, in the eleventh century, another man renowned for piety, the monk Anselm of Bec, was asked to provide such 'flowers from the psalms' for a great and devout lady, he sent her something more. What caught and held the interest of the eleventh century was not Anselm's selection from the psalms, which were quickly dropped, but those majestic prayers and meditations arising from them which gave a new form to the prayer of compunction and tears.[48]

The needs of society expanded the content of monastic prayer and the monastic Office provided, in various ways, a basis for non-monastic personal prayer. For the monks, a steady, unchanging structure for prayer—by the day, by the week, by

---

[48] Cf. St Anselm, *Prayers and Meditations with the Proslogion,* trans. with introduction by Benedicta Ward, Penguin Classics, Harmondsworth, 1973 and 2006.

the year—meant that the monk could absorb the Word of God in the scriptures into his physical mind and memory. It was primarily meant to be a structure for a living faith in a monastery where everyone stayed virtually all the time. The monastic office has always been changed slowly by its users.

No one is born a Christian or a monk, and the movements of the world of time affect each one. But in the West the monastic pattern did not remain the only pattern for religious life. The explosion of clericalism had changed the structure of the Offices, as had the need for mission. From the thirteenth century onwards other forms of religious life were created in the Orders of Friars, Franciscan, Dominican, Carmelite, and later the Jesuits. These changed the shape of the hours of prayer radically, adapting them to the new demands of intellectual study, doctrinal clarification, legal and missionary endeavour, as well as to works of practical charity. It was these Orders which created the breviary, a small book containing the whole Office. In a monastic choir, there was one book with all the lessons in it, another book with all the antiphons in it, yet another with all the collects in it, as well as the Book of the Psalms. Obviously these fitted the stable singing of the Office in choir. In the thirteenth century the friars were constantly travelling, and needed another kind of book. The invention of the minimum in one handy volume says quite a lot about the later approach to the Office. It was no longer the focus of the prayer of the whole body, but the obligation of the individual.

Finally, what then is the value of the Office today?[49] After so many centuries monks today are in some ways in a different position from anything discussed so far, and this for practical as

---

[49] One of the best versions of the Office for non-monks is Morning and Evening Prayer contained in the *Book of Common Prayer* of the Church of England.

31

well as for theoretical reasons. There are mundane things which place everyone in a different position from the past, for instance universal literacy, vernacular translations, printing, and electric light, heating and false teeth. We can now be heard quite easily and we can read what is in front of us. It is, of course, a fantasy to say that we all read—quite a lot of us don't, quite a lot of the time—but it is a different position when we assume that we all can. We no longer need to learn things by heart and so we no longer know the psalter so well that we ruminate on it constantly, unless that happens to be our way of prayer. It is there, printed in the book, and all we need do is go and look at it. Moreover, the change from memorising to reading has meant that different texts can be compared; this creates a new style in criticism of the scriptures which cannot be ignored. Most choirs have adopted two-choir singing for almost the whole of the Office, as a result perhaps of being able to read. This means that during the Office everyone is active, doing something, saying something, ninety per cent of the time, instead of listening and entering into the prayer of the psalms by hearing them in silence from a reader.

But for the monk the tradition of the corporate prayer of the Office remains steady and relevant. If one accepts the call to pray without ceasing as the central theme of monastic life, the hours of corporate prayer still assume their place in the whole ordering of life as a basic part of a discipline. To concentrate on the inner work of conversion of heart in all the ways of monastic life, gives the corporate Office not less but more value as the structure and pivot of each day and night.

What is the value of the monastic office today for those outside the monastery? The office of the monks belongs to time, to this world. It is one of the ways *to sanctify time*—it makes real and active the word of God here and now through the scripture of the psalms. The Office, from the point of view of those attending it, is already arranged, it is therefore an *objective structure* which is not at the mercy of the changing ideas of one or two people. This makes it easily available. It is a stable place of *corporate prayer for the world* where it is known that all attention is given to the work God is doing in the body of Christ. The monk is to become someone open to the indwelling of Christ who is the only One 'by whom the world is kept in being'. Therefore, it is true that the corporate prayers the monastic says in the Office are 'for the life of the world'. But it seems from these early texts that the monk is always very cautious indeed about making such a claim for himself. If he does, it makes him self-conscious and can give him a confidence in the 'good works' he is doing, which can only limit the effectiveness of his whole life of conversion. Perhaps one of the problems for monastics is that we live in a culture where there is no general awareness of the monk's function as one who prays within the Church and the world. So we have at times to become both the ones who do it and the ones who explain it; it is as our own apologists that we stand in the greatest peril.

But the monastic use of the psalms points to an older connection between monk and non-monk—*the psalter is for all.* This is true not only of corporate recitation with others but of prayer when alone doing whatever the work of God is for each. It not only provides a link to the long tradition of Christian prayer, but also gives immediate support in the life-long task of prayer, whether by physical presence or not:

> Let no brother who lives alone in the cell be afraid to utter words which are common to the whole Church. Although he is separated in space from the congregation

of the faithful, he is bound together with them all by love in the unity of the faith.[50]

It may be that some not called to monastic life will use the traditional monastic structure of morning and evening prayer, privately or with others, as a pattern for their daily prayer. However, that is a special choice and is not the only way in which the monastic corporate prayer is of use in the Church. The monastic Office shows an example of the possibility of a unity of life and prayer here and now in time. The details belong to a specific structure of life, but the idea of praying always can be an encouragement to shape other ways of life. Perhaps it is not the content of the monastic office that can help Christians today, but the simple fact of its stability within an increasingly alienated world. Here is a kind of poster showing what is possible for the worst and most lost, since, however bad a monk, however poor the corporate prayer of the monastic community, it still continues as an eternal cry for mercy which is answered by love:

> Now He bids us tell abroad
> How the lost may be restored,
> How the penitent forgiven,
> How we too may enter heaven.[51]

---

[50] Peter Damian, 'On the Book of Lord be with You', trans. Patricia McNulty, in *St Peter Damian*, Faber & Faber, 1959, Ch. 18, p. 74.
[51] 'Christ the Lord is Risen Again', trans. Catherine Winkworth, 1858 from *Christus ist erstanden*, Michael Weisse, 1531, *New English Hymnal* 105.

SLG PRESS PUBLICATIONS
by Sr Benedicta Ward

Recent SLG Press Publications

slgpress.co.uk